ABOUT THE AUTHOR AND THE ARTIST

Michael Harwood is a freelance writer whose principal interests are nature and the environment. The author of a number of books and magazine articles on these as well as other subjects, he lives with his wife in Washington, Connecticut.

Susan Perl is the popular illustrator of many successful books for children—and creator of the marvelous Health-Tex menagerie. Miss Perl lives in New York City with thirteen cats.

REVISED
IMPROVED
EXPANDED

Games

to

TEXT BY

Play in the Car

MICHAEL HARWOOD • **ILLUSTRATIONS BY SUSAN PERL**

CONGDON & WEED, INC. • NEW YORK

To Joslyn and Erica and Lesley and Curtis and Sarah

Text copyright © 1967, 1983 by Michael Harwood
Illustrations copyright © 1967, 1983 by Susan Perl

LIBRARY OF CONGRESS CATALOGING IN PUBLICATION DATA

Harwood, Michael.
  Games to play in the car.

  1. Games for travelers. I. Perl, Susan. II. Title.
GV1206.H37 1983   794   83-1889
ISBN 0-86553-076-9 (pbk.)
ISBN 0-312-92239-6 (St. Martin's Press)

Published by Congdon & Weed, Inc.
298 Fifth Avenue, New York, N.Y. 10001

Distributed by St. Martin's Press
175 Fifth Avenue, New York, N.Y. 10010

Published simultaneously in Canada
by Thomas Nelson & Sons Limited
81 Curlew Drive, Don Mills, Ontario M3A 2R1

Designed by Barbara DuPree Knowles

First published 1967 by Meredith Press

ACKNOWLEDGMENTS

For the ideas and advice that nourished the first edition, I would again like to thank Carl and Clare Brandt, Victoria Chess, George Dickerson, Diane Gilroy, Daphne H. Trivett, Lynne Harwood, Anne H. Layzer, James McGinnis, Judy McGinnis, Michael Melchior, Margo Melchior, Winthrop C. Neilson, III, Geoffrey and Clare Nunes, Betsy Oliver, the late John M. Steele, Jr., David A. Titus, Karen Weed, Peter Weed, and my wife Mary Durant. Several readers have suggested additional games, and three of those games are included in this revised edition; I would like to thank Jean Boetto (who wrote from Illinois), Elizabeth Stonorov (Pennsylvania), and Mrs. Z. Wilkinson (Northumberland, England).

The National Safety Council has contributed rules for safety inside the car. A tip of the hat to the Council for that help and for the rest of its good works.

It continues to be a great pleasure to work with Susan Perl, whose drawings have inspired the author as well as delighted readers. —M.H.

CONTENTS

Outside! Over There!

Break Time

License Plates

Mind Stretching

On Paper

GAMES TO PLAY IN THE CAR

INTRODUCTION

And so Mr. and Mrs. Average Traveler and all the little Travelers have set off on the Great North American Adventure—an automobile trip.

They have been on the road just five minutes, and already Mommy and Daddy know they are in for an awful day. The youngster who is using Daddy's eye as a handhold for climbing into the front seat has just asked for the fifteenth time how soon they're going to "get there." His brother, on the left, in the back seat behind Mommy, is wailing because his tricycle wouldn't fit in the car, and now he has started the *baby* wailing. The other children are quiet, but only for the moment. Soon one of them will tear up a road map and drop the pieces out the window, to watch them blow back on the car behind. Another will pipe up with the suggestion that Daddy stop where everyone can have a

hot dog or an ice cream, and that theme will be repeated and elaborated by an eager soprano chorus. Bladders will fill and throats become parched for a "dinkawatta"—on a maddeningly individual basis. Two separate wrestling matches will start, planting the seeds for progressively nastier rematches throughout the journey. The turmoil will go on and on for as long as the Travelers are on the road.

How can parents and children survive long car trips without crises and crack-ups? Should the children be given a dose of Dramamine and a shot of Scotch each? Should they be bound and gagged? Or do Mommy and Daddy just have to keep yelling at them every thirty seconds to *Behave*?

Such extreme measures are hardly necessary. Games will do the trick—word games, number games, idea games, and travel games. The children may even learn to *enjoy* traveling long distances in a car. This book offers a wide variety of games for them—and you—to try.

In addition to games, some safety precautions and rules of the road will help ensure a sane and enjoyable trip. The most delightful journey would be ruined by an injury to a child—and a lot of journeys are being ruined every year. More than four thousand children age fourteen and under were killed in cars during a recent year, and countless thousands are hurt each year.

In a sudden stop a child can be hurled into the dashboard or the back of a seat. If he is standing up on the back seat, sucking on a lollipop or a pencil or a wrench, a fall could do him terrible injury. It's chilling to see a child lying on the back window-ledge of a car: if the driver has to stop quickly or the vehicle runs into another car, that child may become a helpless, terrified missile. Any hard, sharp-edged toys or auto-repair tools that have been left lying loose can cause serious harm to a child—or an adult—when they are thrown around the inside of a car by the jolt of an otherwise minor accident. When the windows are left open and a child is allowed to put any part of himself or herself outside the car, a passing object—another vehicle, a branch, a telephone pole—can be close enough to injure. Or a

child may lean too far and fall out. These all seem to be obvious dangers, but far too few adults take them seriously enough to protect against them.

The National Safety Council has suggested that parents begin early to teach their children car-safety rules and travel manners, and to enforce them consistently.

RULE NUMBER ONE: *Buckle Up for Safety*. On any trip, whether short or long, a child under five should ride in a child-safety seat, and all older children should put on seat belts. (Of course, adults should set an example by strapping *themselves* in as a matter of habit.) Seat belts offer the bonus of keeping the car interior from becoming a jungle gym. But since they force young passengers to stay put, they cause great problems of priority, dibs, and rights. As everyone knows, not all seats are The Best Seats. One mother says that she gets around this conflict by stopping about once an hour and shuffling the seating arrangement.

RULE NUMBER TWO: *Don't Touch*. Rule number one should prevent a lot of this, but children shouldn't touch the door-handles, the gear shift, the ignition key, or anything else on the dashboard.

RULE NUMBER THREE: *Keep All of You in the Car*. Again, rule number one limits mobility. But hands and arms and heads are not to go outside the windows.

RULE NUMBER FOUR: *Keep the Noise Down*. An uproar in such close quarters is very distracting to the driver, and that could lead to an accident.

There are also a few car-safety rules for the adults traveling with children. Obviously, make sure the car has enough safety seats and belts. Car doors should be fitted with locks children cannot open from the inside. There should be nothing heavy, hard, or sharp lying loose in the car; stow such items in the trunk or the glove compartment, or leave them home. Bring crayons for the children, not pencils. Toys for car trips should be soft—for safety—and quiet—for your peace of mind.

Finally, a word about courtesy—courtesy to the people who live in communities through which you're traveling, and courtesy to other travelers on the road. You should have a firm rule against throwing trash out the car windows. This, of course, applies first to the adults, who must again set an example. Keep a small litterbag in the car, pass it around to the children for contributions now and then, and empty it in trash bins at rest stops.

A FEW BASIC THINGS TO TAKE WITH YOU

Be Prepared. Plan Ahead. To make the trip go as smoothly as possible, take along:

A jug or thermos of something to drink
Paper cups

Snacks (fresh or dried fruit is good)
Paper towels, tissues, moist towelettes
Small litterbag
Soft, quiet, safe toys
Crayons
A watch for timing
Pads of paper or loose paper with stiff cardboard to write on—
enough for all the travelers

And a collection of ideas for imaginative games to play in the
car—to which we now turn.

For

the Youngest

TREASURE HUNT

Before you start out on a trip, sit down with the children and make a list of things to look for along the way. Some samples may be helpful: a broken white pitcher, a burned-down house, a woman wearing a yellow slicker, a hay wagon full of hay, a Great Dane, a blue barn.

Have the children help make up the list. It shouldn't be unmanageably long: thirty items will be plenty. But make sure it includes a few real stickers—like the blue barn, or a white horse with one leg in a cast, or a church with three windows.

Take the list along with you and check off the items as they are found. Any that the family doesn't see can be saved for the treasure hunt on the next trip.

I SPY

One child begins by spotting something—say, a blue truck. He says right away, "I spy, with my eye, something blue." The others try to guess what he saw. If they don't, he gets another chance to stump them. If they do, the one who guesses correctly is *It* for the next round.

The game should be limited to objects seen only outside, or only inside, the car.

STRAIGHT FACE

One child is *It*, and the others invent a phrase for him. Try "the cat's tail." He must then answer every question they ask him with that phrase, and not laugh.

They might ask him, for example, what his favorite breakfast food is, or what he uses to brush his hair, or what would he hold onto if he wanted to make friends with an angry cat, or what instrument would he write with if he had his choice.

The player who makes him laugh is *It* for the next round.

SLEEPING GIANT

The shapes of natural landmarks often remind the viewer of something. Everyone has seen trees twisted into remarkable forms by the wind or by some accident of growth: one might look like a bowing man, another like a woman waving to someone in the distance; two trees can appear to be shaking hands, and another pair, preparing to do battle. Rocks and clouds take on the shapes of human faces, animals, castles, turrets. A range of hills may look like a woman or a sleeping giant. Lots of fun can be had spotting shapes in the passing landscape and naming them imaginatively. No points for this one. Just praise.

ROUND-ROBIN DRAWING

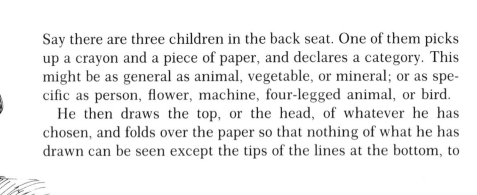

Say there are three children in the back seat. One of them picks up a crayon and a piece of paper, and declares a category. This might be as general as animal, vegetable, or mineral; or as specific as person, flower, machine, four-legged animal, or bird.

He then draws the top, or the head, of whatever he has chosen, and folds over the paper so that nothing of what he has drawn can be seen except the tips of the lines at the bottom, to

which the next player must connect his part of the drawing—
the middle. When the second player is done, he folds over the
paper so that only the bottom edge of his portion shows. The last
child finishes the drawing by doing the bottom part.

As many as four or five can play the game; just make the
assigned parts of the drawing small enough.

In Other Words

GHOST

This is a spelling game in which the idea is *not* to complete the spelling of a word. One player gives the first letter, and the next supplies a second letter. After that, each player in turn adds a letter, while trying not to complete a word—for example, by adding a *t* to *qui*. Any player who, in his turn, adds a letter that completes a word becomes part of a *ghost*—first a *g*, then *h*, and so on—until he's a full-fledged *g-h-o-s-t* and out of the game.

Whenever a player adds a letter, he must have a word in mind that his letter fits. If someone, for example, adds a *q* to *qui*, the next player in line may well doubt there is any word beginning with *quiq* and has a right to challenge. If the player who called the *q* hasn't got a word in mind, he must add a letter to his *ghost*.

The point is to try to force someone else to finish the word, not just to avoid finishing it yourself. If you add a *c* to *qui*, for example, the next player will have to give up or add the *k* that makes *quick* or the *a* that makes *quica* (a small South American opossum)—unless he can think of *quiche*, add the *h*, and pass the problem on.

WORD-PLAY

This is an educational word game. The children identify words on signs along the road that are not words at all. For example: *Ta-kome, Bar-B-Q, Gifts-'n'-Things, An-T-ques.*

There are literally thousands of such obvious distortions of the language, frequently appearing as brand names and as adjectives glorifying various products.

Points are given for proper identification of non-words and subtracted when accepted words are called as non-words.

A somewhat similar game involves spotting unusual names of restaurants, bars, motels, and the like along your way. Points are generally given according to a consensus of the occupants of the car.

The Ho Hum Motel and the Dew Drop Inn may be worth only a few points each, but how about The Tank-and-Tummy? The Zig-Zag Bar? The Morpheus Arms?

MANY OUT OF ONE

An adult thinks of a long word—say, "misunderstand," or "complimentary." The children write it down. (Make sure they are spelling it correctly.)

The game is for each of them to make as many words as possible out of the single word you have chosen. The child with the most words at the end of a certain period of time wins.

You can make it a rule that the words have to be at least a specified number of letters long—three, four, or five. Or you can vary the rules for individuals, depending on the relative ages of the children playing. A six-year-old could be allowed to use any word; an eight-year-old might have to find words three letters long or longer; a twelve-year-old might be allowed only five-letter or longer words.

SMITH TO JONES

The point of this game is to change one word to another—for example, *Smith* to *Jones*—one letter at a time, in as few steps as possible. Like this: *Smith - smite - suite - suits - slits - slots - soots - foots - fools - foils - boils - bails - baits - waits - wants - wanes - janes - Jones*.

Any two words will do. Just make sure they have the same number of letters; five letters is a good size. Crayon and paper are a necessity.

A simpler variation involves asking the children to change one word to another in a specified number of steps: *pale* to *done* in three steps (*pale-pane-dane-done*); *make* to *sold* in four steps (*make-male-mole-sole-sold*).

Scratch paper is legal in this version, but the game is (naturally) more challenging without it. Non-driving adults, who will be preparing the problems, will find the paper indispensable.

BACK-TO-FRONTERS

Someone chooses a word or phrase of two or more syllables, and gives it a tricky, reverse "definition." If the word is "nightmare," for example, the clue could be "day stallion" or (if you believe that mixing languages is fair) "morning ocean." "Heavens, she let 'im go" would lead to "helicopter." The definition "Decent fellow disinters coffee" represents "Cadbury's chocolate." "Old trousers" hints at "New Jersey."

Two things are clear about this game. It is bound to stir frequent debates over the fairness and appropriateness of clues. And it requires as much ingenuity of the person who thinks up the word or phrase and the definition as it does of the people trying to make sense of that definition.

Outside! Over

There!

WHO LIVES THERE?

Most of the trouble that develops with children on a long trip is the result of their confinement in a small space. It is a much closer world than normal, with everybody's elbows and temperaments poking at them. So it is a good idea to direct their eyes and minds outside the car. Who Lives There? is one good way to do it.

Spot a house beside the road—a house with character—and point it out. "Who lives there?" is the question, and the children have to use their powers of observation and imagination to answer it. After the car has passed the house (you might stop for a minute to look closely), they should describe what it looks like inside—what kind of wallpaper, floors, furniture, kitchen, and so on, it has; who lives in it; such details as what they look like, what careers they have, whether they are rich or poor, sad or happy, and why. . . .

Parents should not contribute anything but the choice of house and a few leading questions. Nothing can squash the excitement of this exercise quicker than the imposition of parental wisdom and experience.

Playing the game at night adds a dimension to it, because you can frequently see the insides of lighted rooms as you pass.

A POSSIBLE VARIATION: Who Goes There? using interesting-looking cars traveling along the road.

WHAT KIND OF PLACE IS THIS?

As you pass through towns and small cities—or even states—certain questions may occur to you. How old is the community? Who lives here? How do the inhabitants feel about and treat it? Is it well-to-do, or poor? What kind of businesses dominate it? Where did it get its name?

Here again, parents should restrain themselves. But in this variation small children may benefit from some help in observing and identifying. For example, they may not be able to judge a house's age, even roughly, which would give a clue to a town's age. They may not think, at first, of what dirty, littered streets say about a locale's prosperity or self-respect. A preponderance of motels, antique shops, and roadside stands offering local crafts and farm produce indicates a large tourist trade, but the children may not have any concept of what a tourist is. Smoke-stacks may just be smokestacks to them, not markers of mills, and a feed store in farm country may not mean anything at all. So, if they seem to be having difficulty, make a few connections for them as you go along to get them on the right track.

BEAVER

Pick a target—men with suspenders, for instance. Call it "Beaver." A player scores a point whenever he is the first to spot a man wearing a red shirt.

Once a particular Beaver is called, no one else can call it. Points are lost for repeats and incorrect calls.

Suppose your Beaver is white Cadillacs, and as your car passes one, a player claims it. From then on, everyone has to be careful about white Cadillacs that pass *you*; one might be the same Cadillac and cost the caller a point.

Or suppose the Beaver is houses without any window shutters visible from the road. The two sides of the house in view as you approach it are shutterless, and someone calls, "Beaver." If the third or fourth side, as you go by, proves to have shutters, the caller loses a point.

ALPHABET

Find the letters of the alphabet, in order, on license plates and roadside signs: *a* first, then *b*, then *c*, and so on. First player to get through the alphabet wins.

Alphabet has to be played on the honor system, since the only way to win is to see letters others don't spot; you can't let on where you are in the game. (This will help keep the children quiet for a while.)

The two letters hardest to find are *q* and *z*, and if you're away from urban areas (where this game moves along very quickly) you can get stuck on *q* for an hour, while *r*'s and *s*'s and *t*'s go whipping by.

ONE VARIATION: Do the alphabet backward.

ANOTHER: Limit the game to letters seen on license plates.

TIME-AND-DISTANCE

When you are on a stretch of road where you can see ahead for a considerable distance, pick a landmark near the road and take a poll of your passengers: How far away is the top of that hill (or that water tower, bridge, tollbooth, or whatever), and how long will it take us to get there?

Make a note of the numbers on the mileage indicator and of the time, and then note them again as you pass the landmark. You might give a small prize if one child proves to be closest on both counts, and another for being closest on only one. Double the prizes for guessing the figures on the nose.

NATURE LIST

Keeping a nature list on every trip is a good family enterprise. Note down each kind of animal and plant you see and recognize. (Take with you, if you really want to be serious about it, at least one pair of binoculars and a set of nature guides to help you identify unfamiliar species.)

Some of the listing can be done from the car—of common mammals, flowers, and trees, and of birds with easy-to-spot characteristics, such as crows, robins, blue jays, and mockingbirds with their flashing white wing- and tail-spots.

But more can be seen if you stop from time to time for a rest by the side of the road. Get out, stretch the legs, do a bit of nature-walking.

Continue adding to the list after you reach your destination and also on the way home. Each trip, try to set a new family record for numbers of species recognized.

CEMETERY

Cows make good "pieces" for this game. There's a point apiece for every cow seen, and five points for every all-white (or all-black) cow. Two children, or two teams of children, can play, each team taking one side of the road.

If someone claims a cow that is not a cow it costs him a point. Claiming a one-color cow that turns out to have a spot of marking costs five penalty points. And when the car passes a cemetery, the player or team on that side of the car goes back to zero. Set the winning point score according to how common cows are in the area, or give the game a time limit.

Other possible pieces: dogs, horses, sheep, cats. By the seashore gulls would count a point, and hawks or eagles, five. In farm country, people on foot count a point apiece, those sitting on farm machinery that is not moving, five points. There is no limit to the variety of pieces you can use.

ANIMAL CRIBBAGE

In this game certain point values are given for different animals.
A cow might count one, a rabbit two, a woodchuck three, a deer
four, a fox five, a moose ten. That's an example based on driving
in New England; since the comparative rarity of animals differs
widely from region to region (and since some families will have
certain special animal interests), you will probably want to set
up your own list and point values.

As with Cemetery, the children divide up into two groups,
each scoring on its side of the road. If an animal is seen crossing
the road, whoever calls it first gets it. Fifty or one hundred wins.

AUTO-MAKES-AND-MODELS

It's astonishing that *anyone*—and particularly children—can distinguish between dozens of car makes and models, and remember all the names. But some are whizzes at it, and this game is for them.

One by one each player challenges another to identify a specific car in view. Misses each cost a point, and ten minus points put a player out. The challenger should be able to identify the car himself; if the challengee can't make the identification, he can demand the identification from the challenger, who loses a point himself if he can't answer correctly. (The game can be limited to American, or foreign, cars.)

To avoid unsolvable arguments, it's a good idea to pick cars you can see long enough to verify the make.

— AND YEARS

A variation—but for experts only—is played the same way as above, except that the production year must be included in the answer.

Break Time

EXPLORE

You've been driving on the highway for two hours since your last break, and it's beginning to tire everyone.

Instead of just pulling off at the next rest stop and guzzling soft drinks, pick out a back road on the map—a road that avoids big towns and from which you can easily make your way back to the highway—and get on it.

Be sure to watch your speed. The idea is to change your pace, just as you would if you made the rest stop on the highway. Stop and look at the scenery. Buy the fixings for a picnic lunch. Hunt for something that someone in the car wants to see. Add to the nature list, if you are keeping one. Take some photographs. Stop by a brook and just watch it flow, or let the kids go wading. Relax.

License Plates

LISTING

Probably the most familiar license-plate game is the collection of states, provinces, territories, and foreign countries. There is a checklist of them, for North American driving, at the back of this book. The family can play this either as a cooperative venture or in competition.

A POSSIBLE VARIATION: Pick states, provinces, territories, and countries that will be rarely represented where you travel, and collect *them*, giving points on a sliding scale, depending on how rare you think each will be.

A good place to check for plates, incidentally, is restaurant and motel parking lots along the highway.

Choose a word—say, a child's name, or the name of the next town. Set the children to spelling it out with letters found on license plates.

Of course, the letters must be found in proper order: for "Tuscaloosa," first the t, then the u, then an s, then the c, and a, the l, two o's, an s, and another a.

Set a time limit. If the children are spelling out the name of the next town, they must finish before you get there.

CONSECUTIVE NUMBERS

This game can be played alone or in competition. Start with the number 1, and find it on a license plate; then 2, 3, 4, and so on. Needless to say, this becomes difficult after double figures are reached. A goal—50 or 100 or 253 or whatever—or a time limit may be set, but that isn't required. The count should be kept silently.

NOTE: When traveling on a highway that has a divider strip, passengers on the side nearest the oncoming traffic have a distinct advantage. If this game is being played competitively and you're on a divided highway, rule out all oncoming cars. However, when the road is narrower and everyone can see the license plates on the cars coming toward you, then they can be used.

One version of the game allows the players to use numbers seen anywhere along the road—on billboards, speed-limit signs, the sides of trucks, and so on—not just on license plates.

PICK A NUMBER

Pick a number three or four digits long. Let's say, 1983. Then find it as a registration number or part of one—either in scrambled form, like 3198, or as a natural—1983. Give a point for each version, plus a five-point bonus for spotting the number as originally called for, and an extra five-point bonus if that number turns up all by itself without other figures at either end. Ten points wins.

VARIATIONS: Points can also be given for the lowest-numbered plate on a specified stretch of road; for number pairs seen on license plates, for three of a kind, four of a kind, and for straights or runs (12345, 98765, 14352). Some families compete to find the best poker hands, and others look for cribbage hands.

Palindromes can be used, too: numbers that read the same backward as forward (6116, 232).

LETTERS AND WORDS

This one uses letters rather than numbers. Many registration "numbers" now include a series of letters—for example, a New Jersey plate might begin with "SHK." The idea is to make the longest possible word by using the letters you spot, in order of appearance. SHK can be elaborated into:

SHooK   SHoemaKer   flaSHbacK   SaltsHaKer   SHishKebab

Try a few more sample combinations:

DKD = DunKeD, DicKereD, DrunKarDs
SY = SunnY, SYntax, SYmphony, SYmpathetically
KPC = KnaPsaCk, KlePtomaniaC
BR = antidisestaBlishmentaRianism. Beat that!

The letters must be used in the order in which they appear on the license plate. Thus, with KPC, "back-pack" would not be a legal word, because a *c* appears in the word before the first *k*.

You can use hyphenated words or not, as you see fit. You could make it a car rule that the word has to begin with the initial letter on the license plate, or that it *cannot* begin with that letter. The game could also be elaborated to require that after you've gone as far as you can with SHK or KPC, you reverse the order of the letters and start again, with the highest *combination score* the goal.

One suggestion for a spectacular elaboration of these license-plate games, particularly if you keep score: play more than one at a time. As a matter of fact, why not play them all?

Mind Stretching

BUZZ

Choose a number between 1 and 9—for example, 6. That's the buzz-number. Start counting around the "circle" of players—the first player saying "One," the next player saying "Two," and so on. The catch is that every time the buzz-number comes up in sequence—either by itself or as part of a larger number (6, 16, 63, 426)—the entire number must be replaced by the word "Buzz." Players are out if they forget to say "Buzz" at the right time, or if they say it at the *wrong* time.

FIT AS A FIDDLE

Everyone is familiar with expressions like "happy as a lark," "stubborn as a mule," "dark as the inside of a coal miner's hat." This game is based on such pithy and colorful expressions. Each player in turn is *It*, and must think of a simile—either a common one or an original. Then he states the simile, leaving out the first word. For example, he might say "——— as a lark." The next player has one chance to guess the left-out adjective. If he misses, the player next to him tries it, and so on. The player who thought up the simile gets a point for every miss, and a bonus of three points if everyone strikes out. Twenty points wins.

Creating original similes is challenging, but fun. A few samples to get you started: "Nervous as a mouse in a cat orphanage." "Active as a sand flea." "Pretty as a rose at sunset."

CONCENTRATION

If the driver is getting drowsy, a good, fast game of Concentration, played by the children, will wake him up.

This is a game played to rhythm—one, two, three, four: slap knees, clap hands, snap the fingers of the left hand, then of the right. Everybody does it together—not too loudly. It should sound something like this: *"Slap, clap, snap, snap"*—one beat apiece.

That's just the basis of the game. To the rhythm and action the players add another pattern, a spoken one, and they have to coordinate the patterns without getting confused—rather like patting the top of the head and rubbing the stomach at the same time.

There's no better way to demonstrate how it goes than to give a sample scenario:

FIRST PLAYER:	(*Slap, clap, snap*) "Names of" (*snap*)
	(*Slap, clap, snap*) "automobiles" (*snap*)
	(*Slap, clap, snap*) "Ford" (*snap*)
SECOND PLAYER:	(*Slap, clap, snap*) "Chevrolet" (*snap*)
THIRD PLAYER:	(*Slap, clap, snap*) "MG" (*snap*)
FOURTH PLAYER:	(*Slap, clap, snap*) "Volvo" (*snap*)

And so on, around and around the circle. Players are out if they repeat names or get mixed up—and they will. The last player left is the winner.

Any category of names can be used, of course: girls' names, boys' names, baseball players, states, countries, names of family friends and neighbors, colleges. The driver should set the limit on this game. It gets to some people faster than to others.

ROUND-ROBIN STORIES

In a round robin, everyone tells a part of the tale. Each person in the car, in turn, has a certain amount of time in which to develop the story: a minute or two for the younger children, five minutes for older ones and parents.

Start the story with something seen along the way. When the first storyteller reaches his time limit, the next one picks up where the first left off, and so on.

You might require that when each player has finished his part of the story, he chooses something he sees outside the car, which the next narrator has to weave into *his* segment.

The storytelling can go around the circle for as long as you want—until it either reaches a natural conclusion or becomes too hopelessly complicated to resolve. But generally, once around a four-to-six-passenger group makes a good package, and the last player should wrap up the story.

NAME-STRETCH

Here's a nice one for wild moods. Take place names and work them into a sentence, such as:

I bought a *New Jersey*.
Would you please tell the *Bos to n*ock it off?
The footbone *Schenectady* the anklebone.
Herkimer bride, big, fat and wide.
*Housto n*o the answer to that one, but now I don't.
Up *North, Da kota* very necessary in winter.
That Russian's just a ras*Cali fornia*.
Isn't *Eu rope* about to break, Mr. Mountaineer?

North Carolina or San Francisco should present enough of a challenge to keep a ten-year-old quiet for at least fifteen minutes . . . and an adult for half an hour. Don't expect any hints from me. San Francisco, indeed.

GRANDMOTHER'S TRUNK

Grandmother's trunk, in this game, can hold an amazing variety of articles. "I looked in Grandmother's trunk," begins the first player, "and found . . ." What he found, when the game is given its widest possible scope, may be anything beginning with the letter *a*—say, an artichoke. Player number two repeats the introduction plus the first player's article, and adds his own, beginning with *b*. So the game goes around, alphabetically, with each player in turn repeating the growing list and adding a new object. Players are out if they can't repeat the list correctly, or if they can't think of something to add to match their letters. Failure to think of something to add, of course, is unlikely when the rules permit any kind of article into the trunk.

The game can be limited to specific categories, such as plants or fruits or animals, but it is a good policy to choose rather broad categories, especially when younger children are playing. For example, how long does it take you to think of a fruit beginning with an *i*? A *j*? An *x*?

Crazy categories can be fun—for example, slang expressions. I looked in Grandmother's trunk and found ain't, buzz off, cool it, downer, ego-trip, far-out, get into, etc., etc., etc. One variation of the game calls for items like "big, bad wolf" (for *b*) and "cerise-colored high-heeled shoes" (for *c*).

GOING ON A TRIP

This one, like Grandmother's Trunk, is a memory-tester, and it doesn't even proceed alphabetically. The first player begins, "I'm going on a trip, and I'm bringing a ———," and names an article. The next player begins the same way, repeating the first article and adding a second, and so on around the circle. Players are out if they miss something on the list. There's plenty of room for being silly in this one. On the trip a child could bring not only a toothbrush, socks, a pillow, sweaters, and the like, but fur-balls, a cold, poison ivy, Uncle Jack, Pooh Bear, a pocketful of marbles . . .

This is an old chestnut but a good one. Someone thinks of a subject and gives one hint: whether it is animal, vegetable, or mineral, or some combination of these. The rest of the players have twenty questions—phrased so that they can be answered Yes or No—with which to find out what the subject is. A direct guess at the subject counts as a question.

BOTTICELLI

Botticelli is for older children—say, twelve and up—and adults might join in.

One player picks a person, alive or dead, and announces the initial letter of the subject's last name. B—Botticelli, for example. The rest of the group then starts asking questions about the subject. The basic type of question is: "Is he a composer?" To this the first player cannot simply answer No. He must add that the subject is not so-and-so, i.e., some composer whose name begins with B—Brahms, Bach, Beethoven, Berlioz.

"Is he a compiler of famous quotations?"

"No, he is not Bartlett."

"Is he a tennis player?"

"No, he is not Bjorn Borg."

If the player who is being questioned cannot match the what-ever-it-is with a name beginning with B and the person who asked the question can, the questioner then gets to ask a direct question, to be answered Yes or No, such as, "Is he living?" (But if the questioner *doesn't* know the answer himself, the questioning goes on as before.) The game continues in this fashion until the subject's identity is discovered.

A hint: Pick a subject whose occupational field includes other people whose names begin with the same letter. That gives you an out when you are asked in the above sample game, "Is he an artist?" No, he is not Hieronymus Bosch, or Brueghel, Braque, Boucher, or Bellows. . . .

At its best the game *is* difficult. But it does not have to be played at an erudite level. Children can pick ballplayers as subjects, or friends, or characters from TV shows.

ASSOCIATIONS

One of the children covers his ears, and the others put their heads together to pick some person, living or dead, as a subject. Once they have agreed—let's say they pick Winston Churchill— then the one who is *It* starts asking questions. For example: "What kind of flower does this person remind you of?" The other players discuss their answer out loud ("Not a *tulip*! How about a chrysanthemum?"), and from their arguments and answers the one who is *It* begins to form a picture of the subject. He goes on asking such questions as:

"What kind of music . . . ?"
"What kind of book . . . ?"
"What kind of house . . . ?"

                . . . until he guesses the answer.

One of the children covers his ears and closes his eyes, while the others decide who or what he will be for this game—a well-known political figure? a next-door neighbor? a famous animal? a Muppet? a Beatle? When they have decided, he starts asking them questions about this new identity. "Am I bigger than a house?" "Am I a person?" "Am I a movie star?" "Am I alive?" And so on.

He only has three direct guesses at his identity, and five minutes to ask enough questions to lead him to the right answer.

On Paper

SALVO

This is a game for two would-be naval strategists. Each player draws two game boards, each board having one hundred squares—ten down, ten across. The squares are numbered one through ten one way, A through J the other. This makes it possible to identify each square on a board. Make sure all boards are marked the same.

Now, on one of his two boards, each player "places" the ships of his fleet, without letting his opponent see where they are. He has one battleship, and this occupies four consecutive squares—horizontally, vertically, or diagonally. He has one cruiser, which occupies three squares, and two destroyers, two squares apiece.

Having arranged his fleet on one board, each player now plots out his first salvo on his other board, trying to guess where his opponent's ships are. The battleship and the cruiser have two guns each and the destroyers, one, making a total of six shots. The first player calls out his salvo: say, A-6, A-7, B-7, F-3, F-4, F-5. He marks it on his attack board. His opponent must tell him if he has scored any hits—for example, "You have hit my battleship once, and one of my destroyers once." He doesn't tell which shot hit which ship, however. The attacker notes successful salvos on his attack board. Now the second player fires a salvo, and so on, back and forth. A ship is sunk, and its guns lost, when all its squares have been hit. The object, naturally, is to sink all the enemy's ships before your own go down.

If you wish, you can increase the number and variety of ships in the game, and the number of squares on the board. Submarines, for example—one square each—can be used.

CLOSING THE BOX

This is a good time-passer for two or more children. On a piece of paper they make several rows of dots; how many rows and how many dots per row is up to them, but two of them might try, as a starter, four rows of five dots each.

Then each player in turn connects two of the dots by a horizontal or vertical line. The point of the game is to avoid giving your opponent a chance to close the fourth side of a box. Thus, after six turns each in a two-player game, the sheet might look like this:

Soon it will be impossible to keep from leaving an opportunity to close a box. As a player does close a box, he writes his initial in it, and he goes on closing as many boxes as he can in that one turn. When he can find no more to close, he must draw another line somewhere in the game area. When all the boxes are closed, the player with his initial in the greatest number of boxes wins.

NAVIGATOR

Before you leave on your trip, get a road map or a collection of road maps of the area through which you are going to travel. If possible, have enough for every child who wants one. (If you have the common habit of misplacing your map just at the critical moment, this exercise will rescue you.) With a pen you might mark out your route on each one. Or indicate with a circle or a star the starting point, the key turnoffs, the places—if any—where you plan to stop along the way, maybe a few landmarks (rivers, lakes, state parks), and the destination.

On the trip the children can keep track of where you are by drawing a crayon line along the route as you go. If necessary, give them an introductory map-reading course before you start. Encourage them to keep a current fix on your position by watching for such marks as "Welcome-to" town signs, exit numbers, and route intersections. If the driver thinks it's a useful idea, get the navigators to give warning when a turnoff or stop is imminent.

After the trip is over, those of your children who like to save things will have their own record of where you have been and how you got there and back.

GEOGRAPHY

Ask the children to write down the names of as many of the United States and/or the Canadian provinces and territories as they can think of.

There are variations on this theme. Ask them to name not only the states, provinces, or territories, but all their capitals, too. Ask them to list all the states east, or west, of the Mississippi. Give them the name of a state, province, or territory, and ask them to name all the others that border it; or give them the name of a river or other body of water, and ask them to list all the states and territories that touch it.

You'll find lists of provinces, territories, states, and their capitals, and maps of North America on the next few pages.

CANADIAN PROVINCES AND TERRITORIES

Province/Territory	Capital
ALBERTA	Edmonton
BRITISH COLUMBIA	Victoria
MANITOBA	Winnipeg
NEW BRUNSWICK	Fredericton
NEWFOUNDLAND	St. John's
NOVA SCOTIA	Halifax
ONTARIO	Toronto
PRINCE EDWARD ISLAND	Charlottetown
QUEBEC	Quebec
SASKATCHEWAN	Regina
YUKON TERRITORY	Whitehorse
NORTHWEST TERRITORIES	Yellowknife

THE UNITED STATES

State	Capital	State	Capital
ALABAMA	Montgomery	INDIANA	Indianapolis
ALASKA	Juneau	IOWA	Des Moines
ARIZONA	Phoenix	KANSAS	Topeka
ARKANSAS	Little Rock	KENTUCKY	Frankfort
CALIFORNIA	Sacramento	LOUISIANA	Baton Rouge
COLORADO	Denver	MAINE	Augusta
CONNECTICUT	Hartford	MARYLAND	Annapolis
DELAWARE	Dover	MASSACHUSETTS	Boston
FLORIDA	Tallahassee	MICHIGAN	Lansing
GEORGIA	Atlanta	MINNESOTA	St. Paul
HAWAII	Honolulu	MISSISSIPPI	Jackson
IDAHO	Boise	MISSOURI	Jefferson City
ILLINOIS	Springfield	MONTANA	Helena

State	Capital	State	Capital
NEBRASKA	Lincoln	RHODE ISLAND	Providence
NEVADA	Carson City	SOUTH CAROLINA	Columbia
NEW HAMPSHIRE	Concord	SOUTH DAKOTA	Pierre
NEW JERSEY	Trenton	TENNESSEE	Nashville
NEW MEXICO	Santa Fe	TEXAS	Austin
NEW YORK	Albany	UTAH	Salt Lake City
NORTH CAROLINA	Raleigh	VERMONT	Montpelier
NORTH DAKOTA	Bismarck	VIRGINIA	Richmond
OHIO	Columbus	WASHINGTON	Olympia
OKLAHOMA	Oklahoma City	WEST VIRGINIA	Charleston
OREGON	Salem	WISCONSIN	Madison
PENNSYLVANIA	Harrisburg	WYOMING	Cheyenne

INTERNATIONAL REGISTRATION LETTERS

A	Austria
ADN	Aden State*
AL	Albania
AND	Andorra
AUS	Australia*, Papua* and New Guinea*
B	Belgium
BDS	Barbados
BG	Bulgaria
BH	British Honduras
BL	Lesotho (Basutoland)*
BR	Brazil
BRN	Bahrain*
BRU	Brunei*
BS	Bahamas*
BUR	Burma*

C	Cuba
CDN	Canada
CGO	Congo (Kinshasa)
CH	Switzerland
CI	Ivory Coast
CL	Ceylon*
CNB	Sabah (North Borneo)*
CO	Colombia
CR	Costa Rica
CS	Czechoslovakia
CY	Cyprus*
D	Germany
DK	Denmark, Faroe Islands, Greenland
DOM	Dominican Republic
DY	Dahomey
DZ	Algeria

*Where countries are marked with an asterisk the rule of the road is to drive on the left; otherwise drive on the right.

E	Spain, including Spanish Guinea, Spanish Sahara	GBZ	Gibraltar
		GCA	Guatemala
		GH	Ghana*
EAK	Kenya*	GR	Greece
EAT	Tanganyika (Tanzania)*		
EAU	Uganda*	H	Hungary
EAZ	Zanzibar (Tanzania)*	HK	Hong Kong*
EC	Ecuador	HKJ	Jordan
ET	United Arab Republic		
		I	Italy
F	France, and territories	IL	Israel
FL	Liechtenstein	IND	India*
		IR	Iran
GB	Great Britain and Northern Ireland*	IRL	Republic of Ireland*
		IRQ	Iraq
GBA	Alderney*	IS	Iceland*
GBG	Guernsey*		
GBJ	Jersey*	J	Japan*
GBM	Isle of Man*	JA	Jamaica*

K	Cambodia	P	Portugal, Portuguese Timor
KWT	Kuwait	PA	Panama
		PAK	Pakistan*
L	Luxembourg	PE	Peru
LAO	Laos	PI	Philippine Islands
		PL	Poland
M	Malta*	PTM	Malaya*
MA	Morocco	PY	Paraguay
MC	Monaco		
MEX	Mexico	R	Rumania
MS	Mauritius*	RA	Argentina
MW	Malawi (Nyasaland)*	RB	Botswana (formerly Bechuanaland)*
N	Norway	RC	China (Nat. Republic: Formosa)
NA	Netherlands Antilles		
NIC	Nicaragua	RCA	Central African Republic
NIG	Niger	RCB	Congo (Brazzaville)
NL	Netherlands (Holland)	RCH	Chile
NZ	New Zealand*	RH	Haiti

RI	Indonesia*	SN	Senegal
RL	Lebanon	SU	Union of Soviet Socialist
RM	Malagasy Republic		Republics
RMM	Mali	SUD	Sudan*
RNR	Zambia (Northern	SWA	South-West Africa
	Rhodesia)*	SY	Seychelles*
RSM	San Marino	SYR	Syria
RSR	Rhodesia*		
	(Southern Rhodesia)	T	Thailand*
RU	Burundi	TG	Togo
RWA	Republic of Rwanda	TN	Tunisia
		TR	Turkey
S	Sweden	TT	Trinidad and Tobago*
SD	Swaziland*		
SF	Finland	U	Uruguay
SGP	Singapore*	USA	United States of America
SK	Sarawak*		
SME	Surinam	V	Vatican City
	(Dutch Guiana)	VN	Vietnam

WAG	Gambia		WS	Western Samoa*
WAL	Sierra Leone*		WV	St. Vincent*
WAN	Nigeria*			
WD	Dominica*		YU	Yugoslavia
WG	Grenada*		YV	Venezuela
WL	St. Lucia*			
			ZA	South Africa*

TREASURE HUNT LIST

NATURE LIST

DATE DUE

SEP 16 1999

PRINTED IN U.S.A.

GAYLORD